Hillsboro Public Library
Hillsboro, OR
A member of Washington County
COOPERATIVE LIBRARY SERVICES

LEVEL 2

Kamala Harris

Tonya K. Grant

NATIONAL GEOGRAPHIC

Washington, D.C.

For my dad, who encouraged me to follow my writing dreams —T.K.G.

Published by National Geographic Partners, LLC, Washington, DC 20036.

Copyright © 2022 National Geographic Partners, LLC. All rights reserved. Reproduction of the whole or any part of the contents without written permission from the publisher is prohibited.

NATIONAL GEOGRAPHIC and Yellow Border Design are trademarks of the National Geographic Society, used under license.

Designed by Anne LeongSon

Library of Congress Cataloging-in-Publication Data
Names: Grant, Tonya K., author.
Title: Kamala Harris / by Tonya K. Grant.
Description: Washington, D.C. : National Geographic Kids, [2022] | Series: National Geographic readers. Level 2 | Includes bibliographical references. | Audience: Ages 5-8 | Audience: Grades K-1
Identifiers: LCCN 2021035956 (print) | LCCN 2021035957 (ebook) | ISBN 9781426373251 (trade paperback) | ISBN 9781426373572 (library binding) | ISBN 9781426373466 (ebook other) | ISBN 9781426373473 (ebook)
Subjects: LCSH: Harris, Kamala, 1964---Juvenile literature. | Vice-presidents--United States--Biography--Juvenile literature. | Women legislators--United States--Biography--Juvenile literature. | African American women legislators--Biography--Juvenile literature.
Classification: LCC E901.1.H37 G73 2022 (print) | LCC E901.1.H37 (ebook) | DDC 973.934092 [B]--dc23
LC record available at https://lccn.loc.gov/2021035956
LC ebook record available at https://lccn.loc.gov/2021035957

The author and publisher gratefully acknowledge the literacy review of this book by Mariam Jean Dreher, professor emerita of reading education, University of Maryland, College Park, and fact-checking by Michelle Harris.

Photo Credits
Cover (background), Tupungato/Adobe Stock; (foreground), Renee Bouchard/U.S. Senate Photographic Studio/Library of Congress Prints and Photographs Division; header (throughout), sunward5/Adobe Stock; vocabulary art (throughout), vector_brothers/Adobe Stock; 1, Juli Hansen/Shutterstock; 3, Sheri Blaney/Stockimo/Alamy Stock Photo; 5, Rob Carr/Getty Images; 6, Jim Heaphy; 7-8 (all), Courtesy Kamala Harris; 9, Albo/Shutterstock; 10, Tibor Bognar/Getty Images; 11, Courtesy Kamala Harris; 12-13, Hilary Andrews/NG Staff; 13, Courtesy Kamala Harris; 14, BiksuTong/Shutterstock; 15 (UP), Paul Chinn/The San Francisco Chronicle via Getty Images; 15 (CTR), Shutterstock; 15 (LO), D. Ross Cameron/MediaNews Group/East Bay Times via Getty Images; 16 (LE & CTR), Bettmann/Getty Images; 16 (RT), Eddie Adams/AP/Shutterstock; 17, Mary F. Calvert/MediaNews Group/The Mercury News via Getty Images; 18, Aric Crabb/MediaNews Group/The Mercury News via Getty Images; 19, Rich Polk/Getty Images for LACMA; 20 (UP LE), AP Photo/Kathleen Ronayne; 20 (UP RT), Stephanie Connell/Adobe Stock; 20 (LO), Marvin Joseph/The Washington Post via Getty Images; 21 (UP), Justin Sullivan/Getty Images; 21 (CTR), Official White House Photo by Lawrence Jackson; 21 (LO), Helene Rogers/Art Directors & TRIP/Alamy Stock Photo; 22, Nick Ut/AP/Shutterstock; 23, Win McNamee/Getty Images; 24, Daniel Acker/Bloomberg via Getty Images; 25 (UP), Official White House Photo by Adam Schultz; 25 (LO), Jessica Rinaldi/The Boston Globe via Getty Images; 27 (UP), Saul Loeb - Pool/Getty Images; 27 (LO), Olivier Douliery/AFP via Getty Images; 28, Official White House Photo by Carlos Fyfe; 28-29, Tartila/Adobe Stock; 29, Anna Moneymaker/Getty Images; 30 (UP LE), sachin dogra/EyeEm/Adobe Stock; 30 (UP CTR), Sundry Photography/Adobe Stock; 30 (UP RT), lunamarina/Adobe Stock; 30 (CTR), Leon718/Adobe Stock; 30 (LO), Graeme Sloan/Sipa USA/Alamy Live News; 31 (UP), Dmytro Smaglov/Adobe Stock; 31 (CTR), Al Drago/Getty Images; 31 (LO), Tupungato/Adobe Stock; 32 (UP LE), Aric Crabb/MediaNews Group/The Mercury News via Getty Images; 32 (UP RT), Daniel Acker/Bloomberg via Getty Images; 32 (CTR LE), D. Ross Cameron/MediaNews Group/East Bay Times via Getty Images; 32 (CTR RT), zimmytws/Adobe Stock; 32 (LO LE), Maskot/Getty Images; 32 (LO RT), AP/Shutterstock

Printed in the United States of America
21/WOR/1

33614050922763

Contents

Who Is Kamala Harris?

On January 20, 2021, Kamala (KAH-muh-luh) Harris became vice president of the United States. It is the second highest job in the United States after president.

Harris is the first woman, the first Black American, and the first South Asian American to be elected to that office. She hopes children will dream big and work hard to achieve their own firsts, too.

Harris is the 49th vice president of the United States.

Growing Up

Harris's childhood home

Kamala Devi Harris was born in Oakland, California, on October 20, 1964. Her mother came to the United States from India. Her father was from Jamaica (Juh-MAY-kuh).

When she was growing up, Harris's parents marched for civil rights and voting rights. They took her in a stroller to many of the marches. They stood up for what was right.

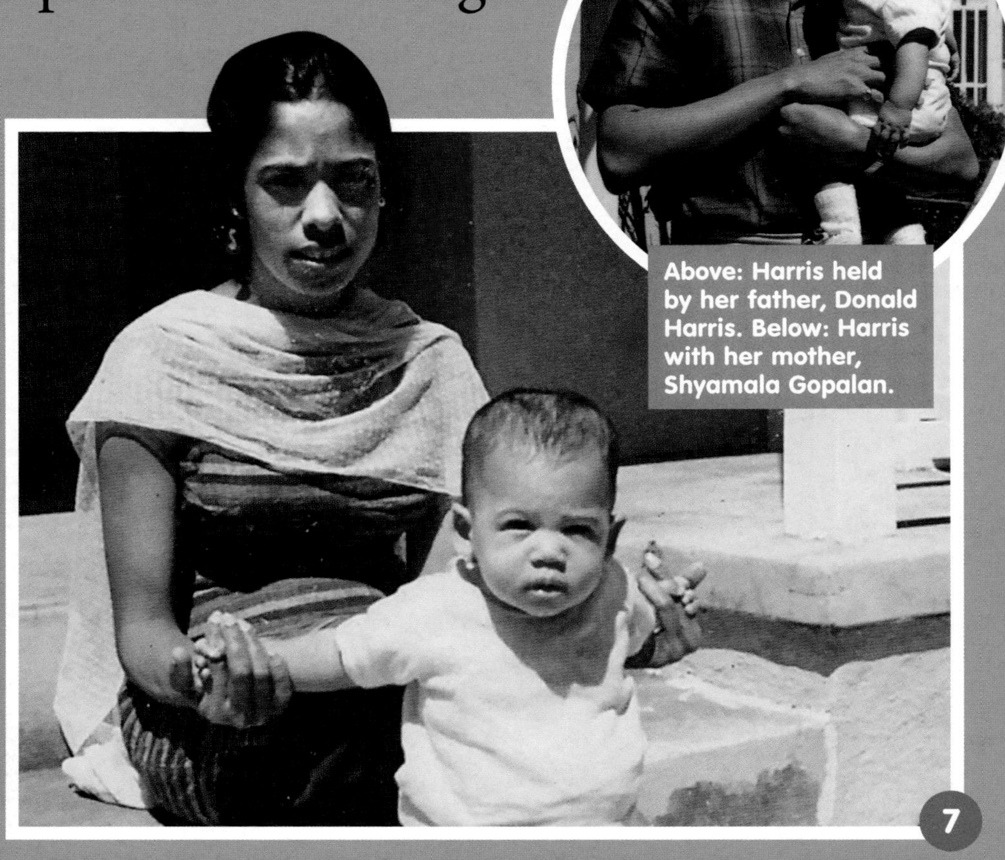

Above: Harris held by her father, Donald Harris. Below: Harris with her mother, Shyamala Gopalan.

When Harris was seven years old, her parents ended their marriage. Harris and her younger sister, Maya (MY-uh), lived with their mother.

Harris with her younger sister, Maya

As a first grader, Harris was part of a program to integrate (IN-tuh-great) schools. Every day Harris rode a school bus to Thousand Oaks Elementary on the other side of town. The program mixed students together. Her classmates there were Black and white, rich and poor.

A school bus from when Harris was young

Everyday Heroes

Harris's family moved to Montreal, Canada, when she was 12 years old. Things were not fair at the apartment where she lived. Kids were not allowed to play soccer on the lawn. Harris thought it wasn't fair.

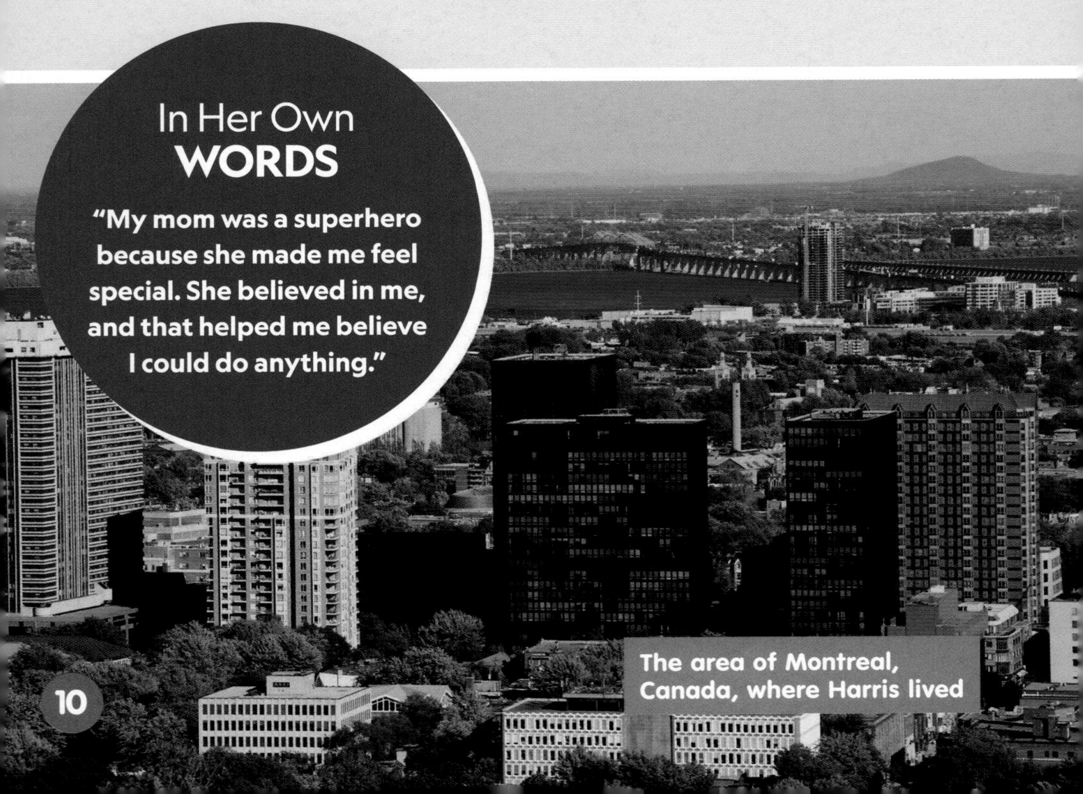

In Her Own **WORDS**

"My mom was a superhero because she made me feel special. She believed in me, and that helped me believe I could do anything."

The area of Montreal, Canada, where Harris lived

Harris with her mother, grandparents, and sister

Harris had learned from her parents, grandparents, aunts, and uncles to stand up for what was fair and right. They were her heroes. So Harris and her sister held a protest. It worked! The building changed the rules. Now kids could play on the lawn.

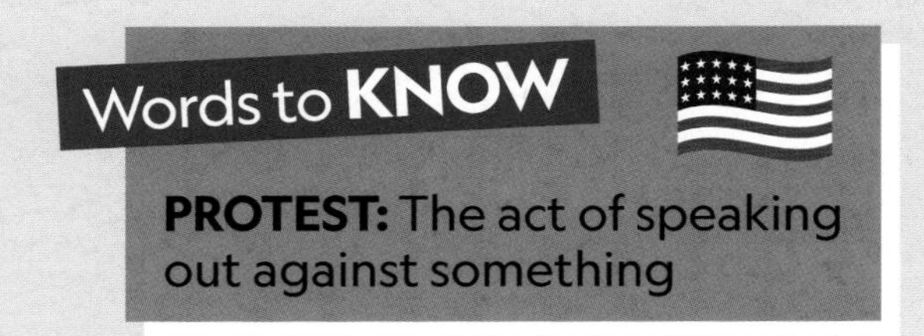
Words to KNOW

PROTEST: The act of speaking out against something

One of Harris's uncles was a lawyer. She knew that people called him when they needed help. Harris wanted people to ask her for help, too. After high school, she decided to become a lawyer like her uncle.

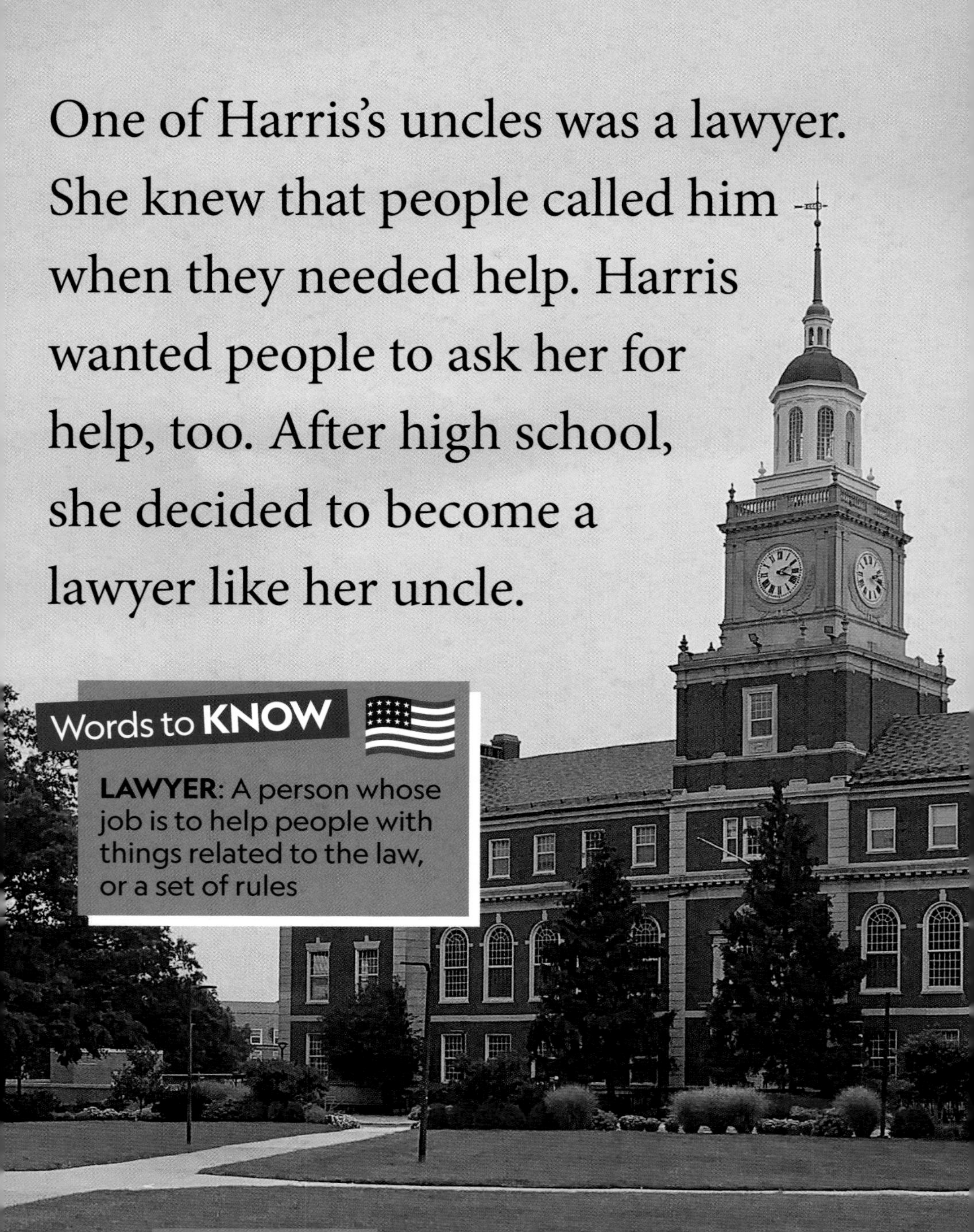

Words to **KNOW**

LAWYER: A person whose job is to help people with things related to the law, or a set of rules

Howard University

Harris went to college at Howard University in Washington, D.C. Then she went to law school at the University of California. Harris graduated from law school in 1989.

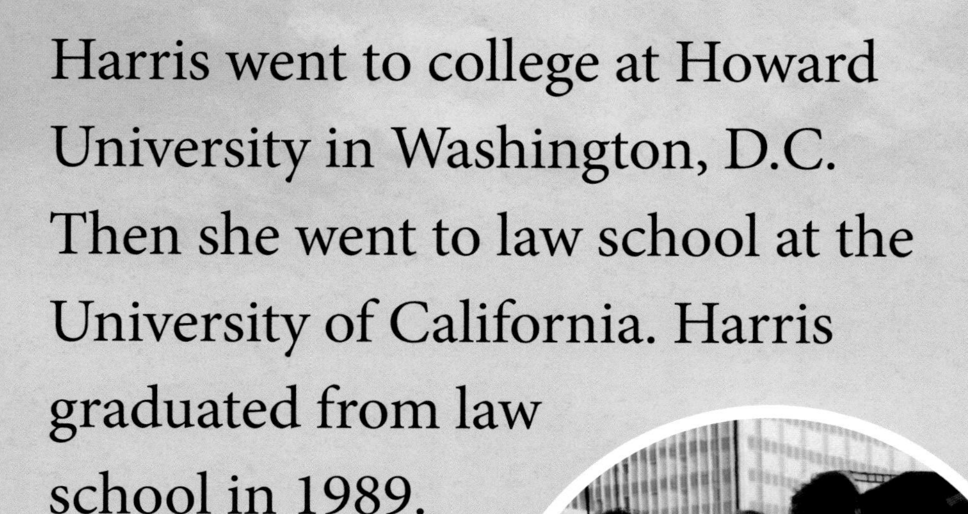

Harris (right) at her graduation from the University of California, Hastings College of the Law

That's a FACT! Howard is a historically Black college and university (HBCU). HBCUs were started to provide a college education for Black Americans.

Harris's Cool Firsts

Kamala Harris was the first to do a lot of things. Did you know these firsts?

2

Harris is the first **Black person** and first **woman** to serve as the **attorney general** of California.

3

Harris is the first **Black woman** and the first **South Asian woman** to serve as the **district attorney** of San Francisco, California.

4

Harris is the first **Indian American** to serve in the United States **Senate.**

Working Hard

Harris failed the test to become a lawyer the first time she took it. But she studied harder and then took the test again. This time, she passed! In 1990, Harris started her first job as a lawyer.

Charles Hamilton Houston

Thurgood Marshall

Constance Baker Motley

That's a FACT! Some famous lawyers that Harris looked up to were Thurgood Marshall, Charles Hamilton Houston, and Constance Baker Motley.

Her job was deputy district attorney in the Alameda County District Attorney's Office. She worked hard to help people. Later, in 2003, people voted to elect her as the district attorney of San Francisco, California.

Words to **KNOW**

DISTRICT ATTORNEY: A lawyer who decides whether to start cases against people accused of crimes in a certain area of the United States

Harris as deputy district attorney

Harris visits an elementary school.

In 2010, Harris was elected attorney general of California! She worked to make sure that all children in California were protected. She also helped win back money for people who had lost their homes.

Words to KNOW

ATTORNEY GENERAL: The chief law officer of a state. They are leaders over many lawyers. They advise the state government on all legal matters.

In Her Own WORDS

Harris's mother would say, "Fight systems in a way that causes them to be fairer, and don't be limited by what has always been."

Harris and her husband, Douglas Emhoff

A few years later, Harris met Douglas Emhoff. He was a lawyer, too. They talked on the phone a lot. They joked and laughed. Then they started dating. They were married on August 22, 2014.

6 COOL Facts About Harris

1 When Harris was running for district attorney, she used an **ironing board** as a desk because it was easy to move around.

2 Harris's first name, Kamala, means **"lotus flower."** It is an important symbol in **Indian culture.** The flower rises above the water while its roots are planted in the ground below.

3 Harris was invited to give a **speech** to students at Howard University's **graduation** on May 13, 2017.

4

Harris **loves to cook.** It is important to her to have a Sunday family dinner. Harris even shares her **cooking skills** and **recipes** online.

5

Harris **loves to read.** One of her favorite **children's books** is ***The Lion, the Witch and the Wardrobe*** by C. S. Lewis.

6

Harris's **pearl necklace** is an important symbol to her. She wears one at almost every important event.

For the People

Harris wanted to help even more people across America. In 2015, Harris began a campaign (kam-PAIN) to run for the U.S. Senate. She wanted the government to make changes to help immigrant children. She pushed for workers to earn more money. She fought to protect women's rights.

Harris speaking with immigrant families

Harris (left) working as a senator

In Her Own WORDS

"I was raised that, when you see a problem, you don't complain about it, you go and do something about it."

In November 2016, the people of California voted. Harris won! She moved to Washington, D.C., to work as a senator. Now she could fight for equal rights for everyone.

Words to KNOW

CAMPAIGN: A series of planned actions to reach a goal

SENATOR: A person elected by voters to represent the people of a state in the United States Senate

Becoming Vice President

Harris with supporters during her presidential campaign

Early in 2019, Harris decided to run for president. It takes a lot of money to run for president. By the end of the year, Harris did not have enough to keep her campaign going.

Joe Biden was still running for president. He wanted Harris to be his vice president. Harris agreed. They campaigned together. The election was held on November 3, 2020. The votes were counted. They won the race!

President Joe Biden and Vice President Kamala Harris

Election volunteers preparing ballots to be counted in 2020

In Her Own
WORDS

"While I may be the first woman in this office, I won't be the last. Because every little girl watching tonight sees that this is a country of possibilities."

Kamala Harris was sworn in as the country's 49th vice president on January 20, 2021. It was a historic moment—one that people will never forget.

It is a vice president's job to support the president. The vice president helps make sure that the laws of the country are followed.

1964
Born in Oakland, California, on October 20

1971
Parents end their marriage

1976
Mother moves family to Montreal, Canada

Harris being sworn in as the 49th vice president

Biden and Harris at the Democratic National Convention

1986
Graduates from Howard University

1989
Graduates from University of California, Hastings College of the Law

1990
Begins work as a lawyer in Oakland, California

Justice for All

Harris's role as vice president inspires many people. Her parents taught her to have the courage to speak the truth. Harris has fought to make changes and help all people. She believes in justice and wants everyone to be treated fairly.

Harris working at the White House

2003
Elected district attorney of San Francisco, California

2010
Elected attorney general of California

2014
Marries Douglas Emhoff

Harris and others clap after Biden signs a law.

In Her Own
WORDS

"I hope that by being a 'first,' I inspire young people to pursue their dreams."

Harris believes that a better future is possible for everyone. She wants children to dream and to know that anything is possible.

2016
Elected U.S. senator representing California

2019
Campaigns for presidency but drops out of the race

2020
Elected 49th vice president of the United States

QUIZ WHIZ

How much do you know about Kamala Harris? After reading this book, probably a lot! Take this quiz and find out.

Answers are at the bottom of p. 31.

1 Where was Harris born?

A. India
B. California
C. Washington, D.C.
D. Jamaica

2 How did Harris and her sister make things fairer for kids in their apartment building?

A. planned a party
B. jumped rope
C. held a protest
D. wrote a letter

Which historically Black university did Harris graduate from?

A. Spelman College
B. Morgan State University
C. Howard University
D. Tuskegee University

4 How many times did Harris have to take the test to become a lawyer?

A. 1
B. 2
C. 3
D. 4

5 What object did Harris use as a desk when she was running to be district attorney?

A. an ironing board
B. a trash can
C. a television stand
D. a chair

6 What changes did Harris want to make as part of her campaign to become a U.S. senator?

A. She wanted to help immigrant children.
B. She pushed for workers to earn more money.
C. She fought to protect women's rights.
D. all of the above

7 What is the second highest job in the United States?

A. senator
B. district attorney
C. vice president
D. attorney general

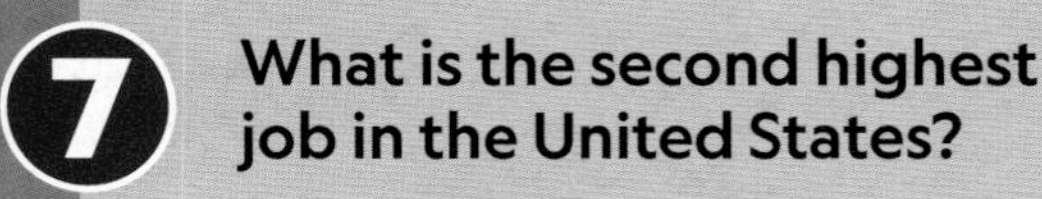

Answers: 1. B, 2. C, 3. C, 4. B, 5. A, 6. D, 7. C